I Had a Job I Liked. Once.

Production Notes

I Had a Job I Liked. Once. was first performed at Persephone Theatre, Saskatoon, Saskatchewan, on 18 April 1991.

Director . . . Bill Glassco
Set and Costume Designer . . . David Skelton
Lighting Designer . . . Luc Prairie
Stage Manager . . . Jane Vanstone
Assistant Director . . . Chris McHarge

Cast of Characters
(in order of appearance)

Sergeant Finestad . . . Jerry Franken
Corporal Heasman . . . Tom Rooney
Les Grant . . . Michael Mahonen
Tracy Tolbertson . . . Cheryl Jack
Tolbertson . . . John Wright

I Had a Job I Liked. Once.

A Play by
Guy Vanderhaeghe

Fifth House Publishers
Saskatoon, Saskatchewan

Cover art and design by Robert Grey

The publisher gratefully acknowledges the assistance of the Saskatchewan Arts Board and The Canada Council.

The author wishes to thank Dan Shapiro for his much appreciated advice and assistance.

Printed and bound in Canada
94 93 92 3 2 1

Canadian Cataloguing in Publication Data
Vanderhaeghe, Guy, 1951–
I had a job I liked. Once.

A play.
ISBN 0–920079–99–7

I. Title.

PS8593.A5386I43 1992 C812'.54 C92–098073–2
PR9199.3.V353I43 1992

FIFTH HOUSE PUBLISHERS
620 Duchess Street
Saskatoon, Saskatchewan
S7K 0R1

***To Bill Glassco**
Without whom this play could never have been written and
would never have been performed*

Characters

Sergeant Finestad, *a policeman in his late forties*
Corporal Heasman, *a junior officer in his early thirties*
Les Grant, *eighteen years old*
Tracy Tolbertson, *a girl of seventeen*
Mr. Tolbertson, *Tracy's father and the local crown attorney*

The main action of the play occurs in **FINESTAD'S** *office in the town's RCMP detachment. There are also three flashbacks, staged with a minimum of props. The time is a night in August of 1967.*

Act One, scene one. *The office of an RCMP sergeant in a Saskatchewan town. It is nearly midnight.*

Act One, scene two. *Somewhat later the same night.*

Intermission

Act Two. *A few minutes following the conclusion of Act One.*

ACT ONE

Scene One

An office in the RCMP station of a mining town in western Canada on a night in August of 1967. The atmosphere is drably functional. There is a door with a frosted pane of glass; on the walls, a blackboard smudged with erasures, a portrait of the Queen. Office furniture consists of a grey metal filing cabinet, large desk and swivel chair, several hard chairs in front of the desk. The desk is heaped with files and ring binders and holds an old manual typewriter, telephone, and desk lamp. Beside the desk is an ashtray stand of the sort found in bus depots, full of cigarette butts.

The curtain rises on **SERGEANT FINESTAD** *seated at the desk. He is middle-aged and slightly rumpled, not slovenly enough to earn a rebuke from superiors, but not quite up to the standard expected of a man in command of a local detachment.* **SERGEANT FINESTAD** *is reading a book with religious intensity and smoking a cigarette. A figure appears on the frosted glass of the door and hovers there for some time as if it is attempting to penetrate the murky glass, then a knock is heard.*

FINESTAD *(glancing up from his book):*
> Just one second, please. *He carefully turns down the corner of the page, closes the book, opens a drawer in his desk, and lays the book in it regretfully. There is nothing furtive about these manoeuvres; he doesn't trouble to hurry. He stares down into the drawer for a moment and then shoves it decisively closed.* Come in.

CORPORAL HEASMAN *enters carrying a clipboard in his hand. He is younger, trimmer, and more military in his bearing than* **FINESTAD**. *His habitual attitude to the sergeant is a mixture of guarded respect and bewildered exasperation.*

1

FINESTAD:
> Tom.

HEASMAN:
> Here are the papers you asked to see, Sergeant.

FINESTAD *reaches out for the clipboard and begins to examine the sheets of paper affixed to it:*
> His Highness is gone then?

HEASMAN:
> Left half an hour ago.

FINESTAD:
> And the Princess Royal?

HEASMAN *shows traces of annoyance:*
> Well, her father left, didn't he? *(A pause.* **FINESTAD** *doesn't look up from the clipboard)* You know, he was more than a little browned off you wouldn't see him.

FINESTAD:
> Then I can't consider my day a waste, can I?

HEASMAN:
> To tell the truth he was right pissed off.

FINESTAD:
> Upgrade it to an unqualified success.

HEASMAN:
> I don't know what harm it would have done to have shown him some consideration. Tolbertson is an important man.

FINESTAD *glances up sharply from the papers on the clipboard. He subjects* **HEASMAN** *to a penetrating look. It is not threatening so much as it is critical and detached. The sergeant does not speak until* **HEASMAN** *shifts himself uncomfortably.*

FINESTAD:
> Tolbertson is *not* an important man. He's a *self-important* man, which is a different thing entirely.

HEASMAN:
> He's a Q.C. and crown prosecutor—

FINESTAD *(forcefully interrupting):*
> Tolbertson is a shifty, two-bit shyster lawyer—titles don't change that. You can sugar shit but when you bite into it, it still tastes of turd. *(He pauses to add weight to what he will say next)* What's more important to remember is we don't *know* that anything happened to his daughter. It's a matter under investigation. I don't bark just because the crown prosecutor rattles my chain, and I don't want anyone else in this detachment to either. *(Pause)* If you get my drift. And I think you do.

HEASMAN:
> Okay, I should have known better than to open my mouth. Seeing how things are so personal between the two of you.

Silence. Suddenly **FINESTAD** *gets to his feet and walks to the blackboard where he takes up a piece of chalk and writes in large capital letters* **NOT PERSONAL.** *He turns to* **HEASMAN** *who has watched this performance uneasily.*

FINESTAD:
> Or do you need a picture? *(Pleading to be understood)* How many times do I have to say it? Nothing about police work is personal. We follow the law, Tom. We're the keepers of the *rules*. If we don't keep them, what right do we have to enforce them?

HEASMAN *(a quiet warning):*
> You're getting a reputation, Jack. For being odd.

FINESTAD *doesn't respond to this.*

HEASMAN *(coaxing):*
> Give this shit a rest. Settle your differences with Tolbertson.

FINESTAD:
> How do I do that, Tom? Because they're big differences. To that bastard the law's a game. He likes to win, so the rules get ignored or bent.

HEASMAN:
> So where's a for instance?

FINESTAD:
> You know how he coaches witnesses. You've been a witness for him. Every officer in this detachment has. *I* have.

HEASMAN:
> Every lawyer goes over evidence with witnesses.

FINESTAD:
> Not the way His Highness does. In the Dirkson case he kept hinting for me to say there'd been an admission of guilt. But I couldn't recall Dirkson making one.

HEASMAN:
> And?

FINESTAD:
> He kept asking was I sure? I told him there was nothing in my notes. He said: "You and I both know, Sergeant, that case notes, due to the circumstances of their recording, by their very nature, cannot be considered absolutely comprehensive or definitive." "Right," I said, "but if somebody *confesses*, that I write down. It's a policy with me."

HEASMAN, *despite himself, laughs.*

FINESTAD:
> Then the oily son of a bitch says: "Very well, Sergeant, we'll leave this matter for the time being and give you leisure to search your recollection for anything you may have overlooked to put in your notes. I don't doubt something will come to you." *(A grim pause)* Tolbertson came this close to asking me to perjure myself so he could obtain a conviction. *(Squeezes*

thumb and forefinger together to demonstrate how close)

HEASMAN:
> Don't go overboard. He asked you whether you had
> forgotten anything.

FINESTAD:
> Oh, the sweet innocence of youth. Or is it?

HEASMAN *(defensively):*
> What's that supposed to mean?

FINESTAD:
> He hasn't helped you to recall anything has he, Tom?

HEASMAN:
> I do my job, Jack.

An extended silence in which the two men study one another.

HEASMAN *(aggressively):*
> Dirkson was guilty.

FINESTAD:
> If I'm any judge of character, I'm sure he was. But that's not
> the point. He didn't confess to me. *(Pause)* Of that I'm surer
> than his guilt.

HEASMAN:
> This one's guilty too.

FINESTAD *shakes his head, walks to the desk and retrieves the clipboard, shuffles the papers.*

FINESTAD *(reading the sheet):*
> His name's Les Grant—this party you've already tried and
> convicted?

HEASMAN:
> Jilly's boy.

FINESTAD *(not paying much attention to Heasman as he studies the complaint):*
    Who?

HEASMAN:
    Old Jilly. We've brought her in a couple of times on drunk and disorderly. She's the bicycle for the beer parlour boys in the over-fifty set.

FINESTAD *(ignoring this continues surveying the clipboard):*
    Who's the father?

HEASMAN:
    Given old Jilly—your guess is as good as mine.

FINESTAD *(looks up):*
    Who's the father, Tom?

HEASMAN:
    Bob Grant. He works out at the mine. He's no joy either, but we've had no official trouble with him. Bad bunch the Grants.

FINESTAD:
    So how many times have we had the boy in?

HEASMAN *(discomfited):*
    I'm not sure.

FINESTAD *(making a zero with thumb and forefinger):*
    About this many, Tom? Would that be a ball park figure?

HEASMAN *nods reluctantly.*

FINESTAD:
    Okay, the boy's never been arrested—never even been questioned by us. So let's go slow and go careful. We'll only do damage by going too fast—damage to the case, damage to the boy, maybe even damage to the girl.

HEASMAN:
> I don't get you. Why wave the red flag at the bull? Tolbert-
> son doesn't forgive and he sure as hell doesn't forget. He
> hasn't forgotten the Dirkson murder case.

FINESTAD:
> What concern is this of yours, Tom?

HEASMAN:
> You think I don't see the strain you're under at home, here
> in the office? It shows in your face, Jack. For chrissakes, ease
> up. You keep going this way, you're going to put a foot
> wrong. And when you do, Tolbertson will see you're out
> of here.

FINESTAD *smiles ruefully.*

HEASMAN:
> What's he asking for? A little cooperation. That's all. I mean
> think, man! He's crown prosecutor, he's a member of the
> town council, and next provincial election he'll run for the
> legislature. Yet every time he asks for something, you offer
> him your rosy red ass to kiss.

FINESTAD:
> Tom, all those things you've reminded me of—aren't they
> exactly what a good cop should make himself forget?
> (**FINESTAD** *opens his drawer, takes out the statute book, and
> lays it on his desk. He taps the cover of the book with his finger*)
> Forget all the rest—remember the law, Tom.

HEASMAN (*making an attempt to explain*):
> The rest of the detachment doesn't understand what you're
> up to. They don't like all this pushing and pulling between
> you and Tolbertson. They feel we ought to all be working
> on the same side.

FINESTAD:
> And you agree with them.

HEASMAN:
Yes.

FINESTAD:
You think I'm the one who's wrong.

HEASMAN:
We think you're wrong. We think you're sticking your nose in his business, putting your feet all over his property.

FINESTAD:
But it's okay for him to try and influence an investigation. Which is what he was up to again tonight. Trying to make damn sure that we lay a charge against this boy—regardless of the evidence.

HEASMAN:
Why would Tolbertson make a false accusation? Lots of people in his position would want to keep this quiet.

FINESTAD:
He's a vindictive son of a bitch, that's why. If he thought some low-rent kid was climbing his fence, picking his apple —

HEASMAN:
Ever think he might just want a bad kid off the streets?

FINESTAD:
What I think is this: Is there enough evidence for a charge? Because if there isn't, we've got no business laying one. Tolbertson isn't bigger than the law.

HEASMAN:
Charge him. If there isn't enough evidence, there'll be no conviction when he comes to trial. Leave guilt to a judge and jury.

FINESTAD:
No. Don't ask me to charge a kid with something like this, put him through the misery of a trial, just to avoid offending Tolbertson. Besides, His Highness can place his own

charge, go before a justice of the peace and lay an information under oath if he cares to.

HEASMAN:
He doesn't want it done that way.

FINESTAD:
No, he doesn't. Because if the police don't press charges, it looks like maybe something's fishy. That maybe this kid didn't do what Tolbertson says he has.

HEASMAN:
Now who's trying the case? You.

FINESTAD:
Bring the kid to see me when he's picked up, Corporal. I'll be here waiting.

HEASMAN (*hesitating, debating whether to divulge what he knows*):
He's been picked up.

FINESTAD (*looks up sharply, surprised*):
When?

HEASMAN:
Twenty minutes ago.

FINESTAD:
Twenty minutes! So, His Highness did light a fire under your ass. Who talked to the kid?

HEASMAN (*reluctant*):
I did.

FINESTAD:
You did. Well?

HEASMAN:
I only had fifteen minutes with him.

FINESTAD:
>And?

HEASMAN:
>He's chippy. A yapper. What you'd expect.

FINESTAD:
>Well the barkers sometimes don't have much bite. What does he have to say for himself?

HEASMAN:
>What they all say. He says he didn't do it.

FINESTAD:
>See the kid in, Tom. I may be looking at a long night.

HEASMAN:
>Let me help you, Jack. Give this one to me.

FINESTAD:
>How could I give it to you—knowing what that would mean?

HEASMAN *(stung):*
>Don't go holier than thou on me. Just remember if any other father came in here tonight and something like that had happened to his daughter . . . you'd have let him talk your ear off. You'd have *listened* to him. How come Tolbertson isn't entitled to what any other citizen is? *(Pause. He points to the blackboard)* What's on the blackboard, Jack? You said police work can't be personal. Maybe you ought to remember that. Because hiding behind rules doesn't make what you're doing any less personal. Jack, you're using the rules to hurt somebody. You give me one reason, one good reason you couldn't have spared him a minute tonight.

FINESTAD:
>The law isn't about pressure, Tom. It's about proof. And if we're getting this kind of pressure now, at the beginning, it could mean there is no proof.

HEASMAN'S *reaction is a mixture of confusion and anger:*
Christ! *(Pulls open the door violently)*

As **HEASMAN** *exits,* **FINESTAD** *shouts:*
Don't forget to send the kid in! I want to talk to the kid, Tom! Tom!

Left alone **FINESTAD** *lets down his guard. He appears tired and depressed. For a time he merely sits, blankly staring into space, frozen. But then he makes an effort to rouse himself, scrubs his face energetically with his hands, attempts to boost himself to his feet using his desk for support. His back kinks and he winces at the spasm of pain. He reaches back with both hands and massages the small of his back, muttering and cursing under his breath. Slowly he straightens himself, gathers up a pile of files, and gingerly makes his way to the file cabinet where he deposits them. He returns to his desk and leans against it, rubbing his back, trying to work the crick out. He seems to improve, tests his flexibility.*

LES *(off-stage):*
First powwow with the Indian, second with the chief?

HEASMAN *(off-stage):*
Watch your lip or I'll powwow you!

There is a knock at the door. **FINESTAD** *visibly pulls himself together, holds himself erect, more erect than is usual for him.*

FINESTAD:
Yes!

HEASMAN *ushers* **LES GRANT** *into the room. The boy's eyes fall on the words scrawled on the blackboard. He finds them a disconcerting puzzle, which increases his tension. His hands involuntarily clench into fists at his sides. He looks away and furtively runs his forefinger back and forth under his twitching nose, a nervous habit he repeats whenever he feels strain. He is eighteen years old, dressed in faded jeans and a faded blue denim jacket. He is bare chested.*

HEASMAN:
All yours, Sergeant.

11

FINESTAD:
Very good, Corporal.

HEASMAN *exits.* **GRANT** *eyes* **FINESTAD** *uneasily. He does his best to look casual, feigns unconcern.*

FINESTAD *(pointing):*
Take a seat.

LES *sits. He nervously rubs his nose until he becomes aware of what he is doing, then he shoves his hand between his crossed legs, pinning it.* **FINESTAD** *settles himself carefully, disguising the discomfort his back is causing him, takes out a pack of cigarettes and offers them to the kid.*

FINESTAD:
Smoke?

LES *fishes out a cigarette and leans across the desk for a light. He tries to arrange himself in a surly, devil-may-care attitude in the chair.*

FINESTAD:
I've been trying to give those up for ten years. *(Beat)* You should quit now before they become too much a habit.

LES *doesn't answer. He blows on the end of the cigarette until it glows.*

FINESTAD:
Anything I can get you? Cup of coffee?

LES *(insolent):*
Uh uh. Might keep me awake.

FINESTAD *(showing no reaction):*
Anything else? Tea? Water?

LES:
Wouldn't mind a Coke.

FINESTAD *leans back in his swivel chair and studies the boy.* **LES**

tries to meet his gaze, loses his nerve, looks around the room, rubs his nose, fidgets. **FINESTAD** *picks up the receiver of the telephone on the desk and dials a single digit. Waits for an answer.* **LES** *watches apprehensively. The conversation that follows surprises and bewilders him.*

FINESTAD:

Corporal Heasman? Sergeant Finestad here. Yes. I've got a request from our guest. Could you step out and pick up a six pack of soft drinks? *(Pause)* Yes, I'm perfectly serious, Corporal. *(Pause)* I know it's late but the China Doll will still be open. Claire can take the desk. *(Pause)* Take the money out of petty cash, Tom, and I'll replace it before I go home. Yes. *(He puts his hand over the mouthpiece of the receiver and addresses* **LES***)* That's Coke, not Pepsi, right? *(Nonplussed,* **LES** *mechanically nods confirmation.* **FINESTAD** *back to* **HEASMAN***)* Yes, Coke, please. All right, Tom. Thanks. *(He hangs up)* Corporal Heasman won't be long. I think we may as well get started. *(He consults his watch)* It's already Sunday. A man shouldn't have to work Sundays. Should he?

LES:

I work Sundays.

FINESTAD:

In my line of work there's no escaping it. But I try to land the four-to-twelve or the graveyard shift on a Sunday. On them I can get to Mass. My wife likes to see me take regular confession and communion. *(Toys with something on his desk, smiles to himself)*

LES *(abruptly):*

How long are you going to keep me here? I'm supposed to be at work by six this morning.

FINESTAD:

Where do you work, Les?

LES:

What's that got to do with anything?

FINESTAD:
> Just a question.

LES:
> Why should I answer "just a question"? When I don't know what it's got to do with anything?

FINESTAD:
> You like your work?

LES:
> Do you?

FINESTAD:
> I used to like it.

Pause.

LES *(despite himself)*:
> I had a job I liked. Once.

FINESTAD:
> Once. *(Beat)* When was that?

LES:
> Summer of '63.

FINESTAD:
> Four years ago. You couldn't have been very old.

LES:
> Fourteen. Fucking old enough.

FINESTAD *(waiting a moment before proceeding)*:
> And this job you liked, where was it?

LES *(abrupt, sullen)*:
> Golf course.

I Had a Job I Liked. Once.

FINESTAD *(flatly)*:
Golf course.

LES:
Yeah, the summer they put in all the bunkers and sand traps. *(Remembering)* The sand had to be just so, real fine, no rocks, or pebbles, so's when some big shot from head office was playing here, he wouldn't catch a rock blasting out of our traps and nick his fucking wedge or whatever.

FINESTAD *laughs.*

LES *(encouraged)*:
Really. But they couldn't find the right sort of sand anywhere. So they had to make it. That's where I come in. You hire a kid under sixteen—you don't have to pay him minimum wage. It's the law. I come cheap. Sixty cents an hour. Least that's what I was *supposed* to get.

FINESTAD *(drawing him out)*:
And you really *made* sand?

LES *(forgetting himself, with pride)*:
Yeah, out in a gravel pit. First I had to pitch gravel against a coarse screen—to separate out the big stones. Then they had this shaker, like a big flour sifter. I fill it up with what's gone through the coarse screen and I shake it and shake it, shake it fine as powdered sugar. I shovel that on a wagon. When I get a wagonful—takes me two days—a groundskeeper pulls it away with a tractor. Then I start over. Making sand.

FINESTAD *(dubious)*:
And this job you liked?

LES *(with feeling)*:
Yeah, it was nice.

FINESTAD:
Why?

LES:
> Huh?

FINESTAD:
> What was nice about it?

LES *(slowly and carefully):*
> Well, I was alone out there, at the pit, see?

FINESTAD *nods.*

LES:
> I liked being alone. And there was all the fresh air and the sun and like that. I got a great tan. Only summer I ever got a decent tan.

FINESTAD *nods and* **LES** *seems to gain confidence from the gesture.*

LES:
> I got so much sun that summer my hair started to bleach on top. *(He fingers it)* I had this Beach Boys album at home—I looked like Brian Wilson. I looked California.

FINESTAD:
> California?

LES:
> Surfer. I bought the ice-cream pants and the candy-stripe shirts to go with the hair, the tan. I had the desert boots. I wasn't the same guy come school in September. I had the total look. *(Pause)* But then—my hair grew back dark and I didn't have money for clothes *(cynically indicating his appearance)* so I went back to being a geek.

FINESTAD:
> So no money—no total look.

LES:
> No money—no nothing.

FINESTAD:

But on the other hand people say money isn't everything.

LES *laughs bitterly.*

FINESTAD *feigns surprise*:

No?

LES:

Can we talk about something else?

FINESTAD:

You don't like talking about money?

LES:

What good did talking about money ever do guys like me?
I talked myself blue in the face to the big shots at the golf
course—didn't mean shit. Nobody listened.

FINESTAD:

I'll listen.

LES *(sarcastically)*:

Listening doesn't cost you nothing.

FINESTAD:

And talking doesn't cost you anything either, Les. So tell
me about the big shots at the golf course.

LES:

Fuckers hired me, they said I get sixty cents an hour to
throw gravel. That was the club manager said that. First
payday I get my cheque—I'm short. "What's this?" I say.
"Oh," he says, "the Recreation Board figures we oughtn't
to pay by the hour, we ought to pay by the wagonload because you're off by yourself without a foreman and nobody knows how hard you work. So we'll pay you by the
wagonload and then we know that we're getting value."
So like I said, it takes me two days to do a wagon so I ask,

"How much a wagon?" And he says, "The board thought
seven dollars a wagon. You want to work hard you should
do pretty good." Work hard. Henderson is on that board
and he pays his kid a buck to cut his fucking lawn. How
long does it take to do a lawn? Know why the big shots pay
their little ass suckers to cut the lawn? To teach them the
meaning of a dollar. How come a dollar doesn't mean the
same thing to me as it does Henderson's kid?

FINESTAD:
So what did you do?

LES:
What do you think? Took seven dollars a wagon. *(Pause)*
What else, I ain't telling.

FINESTAD:
Les's little secret.

A moment of silence.

FINESTAD:
But you've got a different job now.

LES:
Yeah. Swimming pool.

FINESTAD:
Strikes me that the swimming pool would be a step up on
the gravel pit. Sounds like the kind of summer job a young
fellow would give his eye teeth for. Sounds glamorous.

LES:
Right. It's the cat's ass.

FINESTAD:
Sitting up there high on that lifeguard's chair with the best
view of the bathing beauties, working on your tan. The high
life with pay.

LES:

Hey, what is it with you?

FINESTAD:

Me?

LES:

I'm maintenance. I'm pump room. Cold dripping pipes and sticky valves and chlorine to make your eyes water. I'm no asshole lifeguard. The lifeguard's chair belongs to the university boys. They got dibs on the high chair. Their daddies barbecue with the big shots. My daddy don't barbecue with nobody. He's no chum of theirs. *(Pause)* Me either, unless they need to bum a smoke.

FINESTAD:

So who are your friends, Les?

LES:

Huh?

FINESTAD:

Who do you hang out with?

LES:

You mean at work?

FINESTAD:

Anywhere.

LES:

At work with Old Mike. We get ten minutes off—we hang out at the window with the grill. *(Suddenly laughs to himself)* Old Mike loves the girls. He's got to be sixty but he still acts the tail hound. He says all those brown girls, all different shades of brown, they put him in mind of a box of assorted chocolates. He says he'd like to taste them all.

FINESTAD:

And what do you say, Les?

LES:

> I say I got about as much chance with one of the "assorteds" as Mike does. That's expensive chocolate.

FINESTAD:

> But you like to look.

LES:

> No harm in looking.

FINESTAD:

> You ever ask one of these girls out, Les? Ever ask them for a date?

LES:

> Get serious.

FINESTAD (*feigning surprise*):

> You never asked one of them out?

LES:

> No.

FINESTAD:

> So (*pretending to fumble for the name*) what's her name? This Tracy Tolbertson—she's not chocolate?

LES *doesn't respond.*

FINESTAD:

> Now I'm no expert on what you and Old Mike call chocolate but I've seen this young lady a few times—just a few mind you—and I'd put her down as chocolate. Yes, I would, Les. Pricey chocolate.

There is a knock at the door. **FINESTAD** *doesn't take his eyes off* **LES'S** *face.*

FINESTAD:

> Come!

HEASMAN *enters carrying a carton of Coke. His dignity is offended at being made to act the errand boy. He glares at* **LES** *as he passes by him on his way to deposit the drinks on the desk.*

FINESTAD:
>Thank you, Tom. I'm sure our guest appreciates your trouble. He's been telling stories—really interesting ones—and I believe if you hadn't arrived right now with refreshment he might have gone dry on me. *(Beat)* But once Les wets his whistle I'm sure we'll be off and running once more. Am I right or am I wrong, Les?

HEASMAN:
>There's more than one way to prime the pump.

HEASMAN *exits.*

FINESTAD *(opens and passes a bottle to* **LES***):*
>Please excuse the corporal. He thinks of himself as a practical man.

LES *(hesitant, anxious):*
>He—him *(***LES** *gestures in the direction of the door)* he said I could get ten years—ten years and a whipping. Is that right, ten years and a whipping? *(He rubs his nose, drinks)*

FINESTAD:
>Corporal Heasman doesn't hand out sentences, son. Nobody in this office does. We're policemen, not judges.

LES:
>That one—he's got it in for me.

FINESTAD:
>No, more likely he's upset with me. We haven't been seeing eye to eye lately. Tom doesn't believe in my chats—chats like the one you and I've been having. But I look at it this way. You can frighten information out of someone, but not

21

the truth. Truth, the genuine article, is a gift. That's why I give everyone a chance at volunteering the truth before I fall back on prying out information. But you and I aren't going to settle for mere information. Are we, Les?

There's a knock on the door.

FINESTAD:
Yes!

The door opens and **HEASMAN** *sticks his head into the office.*

HEASMAN:
Sergeant, you're wanted on the phone.

FINESTAD *(taps his telephone):*
Put it through then, Tom.

HEASMAN *(hesitates):*
I think you'll want to take this one on the desk.

FINESTAD *(concerned):*
Who is it? My wife?

HEASMAN:
Not Irene. *(He looks meaningfully at the boy)* For your ears only.

FINESTAD:
It's Tolbertson then?

HEASMAN *glances in the direction of the boy and then nods.*

FINESTAD:
What does he want?

HEASMAN *(reluctant to speak in front of* **LES***):*
He wants to be apprised of how matters stand.

FINESTAD:
Apprise him that I am conducting a questioning and regret

I cannot come to the phone.

HEASMAN:
> For the sake of peace, Jack.

FINESTAD:
> Tell him, Tom.

HEASMAN:
> You better come. He wants to know what in hell is going on. And he wants it from the horse's mouth.

FINESTAD:
> Tell him to go to bed and get some sleep. Tell him I'll call him first thing tomorrow morning with news when I know how this matter stands.

HEASMAN *withdraws his head and closes the door.*

FINESTAD *(relieved):*
> I thought for sure that would be Irene. Whenever I'm late getting home from work—I figure it's her. Tonight I was supposed to be home just past midnight, but because of you I missed the boat. During the day, if I'm late, I can phone. But at night . . . After midnight, you call and she may be asleep, you may get her out of bed. On the other hand, she could be sitting up worrying, waiting—

LES:
> Who gives a shit?

FINESTAD *(suddenly dangerous):*
> I do. To me it matters if my wife is sitting up, half-crazy with worry. That's nothing to you, a person sick with worry?

LES *stares at him belligerently.*

FINESTAD *(half-apologetic for his outburst):*
> "Quit," she says to me. "You don't need the stress. You're

going grey in the face as a pan of ashes." The woman scarcely draws an easy breath, always phoning me here at work just to make sure nothing's happened to me. But Saturday nights are definitely the worst. She's got this weird idea in her head that something's going to overtake me at the eleventh hour and I won't make Sunday, won't make Mass. (*Beat*) And confession, always after me to go to confession. So that if I'm taken sudden, in the line of duty, I won't go with a backlog of sin on my head. It's crazy. (*Pause*) Sometimes I wonder if she doesn't fret like this over me because we had no kids for her to worry about. (**FINESTAD** *lapses into reverie.* **LES** *observes him closely. Suddenly the sergeant is struck by something. He sits bolt upright*) Damn!

LES (*starting*):
What?

FINESTAD:
Did Corporal Heasman notify your parents that we're holding you?

LES:
Not that I know of.

FINESTAD (*taking hold of the phone*):
Let's have your number then. It's late. They'll be wondering what happened to you.

LES (*dryly*):
Don't get your shit in a knot. The old man is working the graveyard shift. He won't be back from the mill until eight-thirty, quarter to nine.

FINESTAD:
What about your mother?

LES:
Jilly Grant? Jilly Grant Me a Poke? (*He stops himself abruptly*) She won't be home.

I Had a Job I Liked. Once.

FINESTAD *carefully replaces the receiver. He keeps his eyes off the boy's face and the shame evident there. Both are silent for a considerable length of time.*

LES *(angry, desperate to escape his feelings):*
> So what about you? You believe that shit?

FINESTAD *(quietly):*
> What shit's that, Les?

LES *(antagonistic):*
> This Catholic shit of your wife's.

FINESTAD:
> At the start—when I joined the Church—I didn't believe anything. I'm a convert, you see. I did it because my wife . . . Irene . . . I did it because she wouldn't marry me otherwise. Father Johns. He put me through my paces. I knew it all, word perfect. Had to for Father Johns. He didn't trust converts—especially the marrying sort. He had a bad thirst, liked to hoist a jar. More than liked . . . *loved* to hoist one. The Drinking Father I called him.

LES:
> I got one of them too.

FINESTAD:
> He wasn't a bad man. He helped me.

LES:
> Those guys help nobody.

FINESTAD:
> Live a little and you'll learn to take help wherever it's offered. I was young. I needed it bad. Those early years as a policeman were tough.

LES:
> Tough job—writing out tickets.

FINESTAD *(passionately):*

> You want to know what a policeman's job really is, Les?
> He's a one-trick pony. His trick is holding things together.
> And he can never tell what he knows, never let the secret
> out that what the world really wants is to come apart in our
> hands. Because house fires, accidents, scalded babies, mur-
> ders, are all signs of the same thing—the world wanting to
> break. Seeing that day after day I started to feel I was break-
> ing up too. Being pulled apart, bit by bit.

LES *(unsure what this means):*

> So how did Humpty Dumpty get together again?

FINESTAD:

> I started to do what Father Johns said I should. Go to Mass.
> No cigarettes during Lent. Say my rosary. Remember my
> sins and confess them. The rules made me feel solid, kept
> me from flying apart. There are certain kinds of jobs you
> can't do unless you feel that what you face every day isn't
> all there is to it. And that was what was good about the
> Church. It talked about a world above, or beyond, or in
> back of the world I was staring in the face every day. That
> world corrected the mistakes of this one. Father Johns had a
> name for it— City of God. So one day I woke up and real-
> ized I'd swallowed everything I'd laughed at growing up
> Protestant—no meat on Fridays, St. Christopher's medals,
> Latin, confession. I believed. *(Pause)* I can guess why I went
> in that direction then. Who knows why I'm going in the op-
> posite direction now? Every morning I wake up and some-
> thing else is gone. So when you ask me what I believe in
> now—I don't know how to answer. (**FINESTAD** *sits quietly
> for some time. Then he stirs himself, smiles self-consciously)* We
> seem to have got off track here, haven't we?

LES:

> Could be.

FINESTAD:

> Yes. We've forgotten about Miss Tolbertson and all the

interesting questions I had to ask about her. *(Pause)* If I remember correctly, a while ago I asked you if you had ever asked one of those girls—like Tracy Tolbertson— to go out with you, and you said you hadn't. Did I get that right, Les?

LES *(on the defensive once more):*
Yeah.

FINESTAD:
But she was in your car tonight, wasn't she?

LES *doesn't answer.* **FINESTAD** *waits for a moment.*

FINESTAD:
Was she or wasn't she in your car tonight?

LES:
Yeah.

FINESTAD *(sharply):*
Yeah she was or yeah she wasn't?

LES:
Yeah she was!

FINESTAD:
And you wouldn't call that a date?

LES:
No.

FINESTAD:
What would you call it?

LES:
I'd call it giving somebody a lift.

FINESTAD:
Or a pickup?

LES *remains stubbornly silent.*

FINESTAD:
How well do you know Tracy Tolbertson, Les?

LES:
Not very. She was in my home room last year.

FINESTAD:
But you saw her outside school?

LES:
Sometimes.

FINESTAD:
Where?

LES *(evasive):*
Around.

FINESTAD:
Around isn't good enough, Les. Where?

LES *shrugs.*

FINESTAD:
Where?

LES *rises from his chair and begins to pace nervously about the office, repeating* **FINESTAD'S** *question in a mocking manner:*
Where? Where? *Where? (He passes the blackboard and snatches up a piece of chalk)* Okay, let me situate it for you exactly. *(He draws a line on the floor with the chalk, points to it)* There's the grill. *(He gestures to one side of the chalk line)* Pump room. *(Indicates the other side)* Swimming pool. *(Stepping to the pump room side of the line he touches his chest)* Me. *(Points to the other side)* Tracy. *(Hesitates)* Them.

Lights create a lattice-work effect to suggest a grill. **LES'S** *demeanour changes. He is now temporarily in the past. He takes several slow steps* *back from the imaginary window.* **FINESTAD** *is watching with close attention.* **LES** *stands absolutely immobile for several moments and then* **TRACY TOLBERTSON** *makes her entrance wearing a two-piece bathing suit. She approaches the imaginary window. From behind her comes the faint sounds of a swimming pool, splashes, the excited cries of children. From* **LES'S** *side there is an undertone of reverberating machinery. It is evident the girl does not see* **LES**. *She cups her hands to the side of her face and peers through the window. She pitches her voice and calls.*

TRACY:
> Lester! Oh Lester! *(She casts a glance back over her shoulder and giggles to an unseen audience of friends. Then she turns back to the window and yodels comically)* Oh Lester, Lester. Come out, come out, wherever you are!

LES *pricks his ears at the sound of her voice, listens intently. Then he begins to move forward stealthily with a smile on his face, wiping his hands with a rag he has taken from his back pocket. It is obvious that he can see her but she still can't see him.*

TRACY:
> Ooooh Lessster! There's a good boy! Come to Maa-maa! *(She glances back to her friends to gauge their appreciation of her performance, laughs and waves. By the time she turns around* **LES** *is standing very near the window but she still doesn't see him)* Lesster! Oooh Lesster!

LES:
> Yes?

TRACY *(starts violently):*
> Oh my God! *(She retreats a few steps with her hand pressed to her heart. Then, cautiously)* Les, is that you?

LES *smiles to himself.*

TRACY:
> If that's you, Les, come up to the grate so I can see you. *(She edges forward uncertainly)* Les? Les?

LES (*moves forward, reaches up and hooks his fingers in the imaginary grate, pretends to mash his face into it*):
>Close enough?

TRACY (*relieved*):
>You deserve a good smack for scaring me like that. Shame on you, Les!

LES (*grinning*):
>What's to be scared of?

TRACY:
>Well, it's so bright out here and so dark back there in that room a person can't ever see in properly and I never know who I'm going to get when I call. It could be that dirty old pervert Mike, Mike Whatsis Name.

LES (*pointing behind him*):
>I didn't hear you at first because of the pumps running. I can always see you though. I can make you out clear as a photograph from way back there, the farthest wall.

TRACY (*kittenish, teasing*):
>And how do I look from way back there?

LES (*ill at ease*):
>Nice. Real nice. You're getting the outstanding tan.

TRACY:
>Nice. Way to be, Les. That's what every finely tooled sex machine wants to hear—that she looks nice.

LES (*laughing nervously*):
>The mouth on you. It'll get you into trouble some day.

TRACY:
>Let's hope.

LES (*anticipating why she has come*):
>Well, I'd guess . . .

I Had a Job I Liked. Once.

TRACY:
> You'd guess . . .

LES:
> You're on the verge of a nicotine fit.

TRACY:
> Severe withdrawal, Les. The severest.

LES (*pulling a package out of his back pocket*):
> I can't believe it. Changing my brand to suit you. You got me on menthols now, Tracy. Candy-ass smokes.

TRACY:
> I'm only thinking of you, Les. They're good for summer colds.

LES (*fumbling with package*):
> I don't get summer colds.

TRACY (*impatient*):
> Come on, butter fingers. I'm dying for a weed. Pass it through the grate.

LES (*pokes a cigarette through the grate*):
> There. You got it?

TRACY:
> I got it. Carry on.

LES:
> Carry on?

TRACY:
> I got friends, don't I? You expect me to smoke in front of friends and torture them?

LES (*looking around her*):
> So who you with today?

31

TRACY:
> The usual crowd. Don and Carol, Susan and Jane . . . Bob.

LES *(disgusted):*
> *Bob.* What's that then? Five?

TRACY:
> Yeah, five more. Make it an even half-dozen and I can have a second.

LES:
> Jesus, that only leaves me with two for the rest of the day.

TRACY:
> Don't be so tight, Les. It's not appealing. Besides, you're working, aren't you? What are the poor unemployed rest of us supposed to do?

LES:
> I've got to be crazy. *(He begins to pass cigarettes through the grate on the window)* Supplying that jerk Bob Marsh with cigarettes.

TRACY:
> Now you mustn't talk like that in front of me, Les. Bob and I are going out together now.

LES *(stops with a cigarette poised in mid-air):*
> Bob?

TRACY:
> Well, it's just a summer thing, I think. Until he goes back to school in Chicago. It doesn't feel permanent or anything. But who knows?

LES *(resumes passing out cigarettes):*
> Bob Marsh. Bob the Bog. Here's his. Hope he chokes on it.

TRACY *(warning him):*
> Les.

LES *(finishes passing them out):*
> There.

TRACY:
> Six. You're a prince among men, Les. *(Pause)* You know I wouldn't always be bumming smokes from you except—

LES *(turning to address* **FINESTAD***):*
> Except it doesn't make any sense for her to buy her own because if her old man caught her with them—

TRACY *(interrupting):*
> Right on the money, Les. You're my saviour.

LES *(smiles, turns back, half-believing her sincerity):*
> Well . . . *(A signal that he should be thinking of getting back to work)*

TRACY:
> Don't run off so soon, Les.

LES:
> I ought to get back. A pump's broken down.

TRACY:
> Talk to me for a second. We were all wondering what you've been up to. Seen any good movies? *(Coyly and mischievously)* Read anything interesting lately? Bob the Bookworm wanted me to ask.

LES *is clearly disturbed by her last question. He tries to ignore it, avoid it. He speaks hurriedly, loudly:*
> I got to go now. I . . . I got work to do. The pump . . . I got to run, Trace.

FINESTAD *has picked up on the significance of this moment. He intervenes, freezes* **LES** *in his tracks with a loud question.*

FINESTAD:
> Read anything interesting lately? What did she mean by that, Les?

LES:
> I don't know. Whyn't you ask her?

FINESTAD:
> Because I'm asking you, Les.

LES *turns back to* **TRACY.** *He looks determined, purposeful.*

LES:
> Who's doing it, Tracy?

TRACY *(acting innocent):*
> Doing what, Les?

LES:
> Writing that stuff on the walls.

TRACY:
> What stuff are you talking about?

LES *(with difficulty):*
> Stuff about my mother.

TRACY:
> Oh, I don't know anything about that.

LES:
> Everybody knows about that. I want to know who's doing it.

TRACY:
> Les is playing detective.

LES:
> This isn't a game.

TRACY:
> Everything's a game, Les.

LES:
> It shouldn't be.

I Had a Job I Liked. Once.

TRACY:

> My old man makes my mother count the china once a week. In case of breakage. She makes a report, so many cups, so many saucers, so many plates. A little power trip to give him his weekly little hard on. That's his game.

LES (*disapproving*):

> Tracy.

TRACY:

> Want to know mine? Perfection. No smoking, no drinking, no swearing. (*Strikes a pose, laughs cynically*) Daddy's little girl.

LES (*obsessed*):

> If you heard who was doing it—you'd tell me, wouldn't you, Tracy?

TRACY:

> How would I hear, Les?

LES:

> Well, you're with people, your friends—out there. And I'm back here, where I'd never hear. But I know people talk, they laugh about stuff like that.

TRACY (*sharply*):

> Don't whine, Les.

LES:

> I mean it's bad enough they write that stuff. But it's me who has to go wash it off the walls. That's my job. *I* have to clean it up. And now . . . now it's in the girls' change-room too.

TRACY:

> I should be getting back to my friends.

LES:

> I wouldn't have thought girls would write stuff like that.

TRACY:
> I don't see why girls have to be any better than boys!

TRACY *begins to leave.* **LES** *calls to her.*

LES:
> Tracy?

TRACY:
> What!

LES *(fumbling to appease her):*
> Your tan's really coming along. It looks great.

TRACY *(running her hands up and down her arms, admiring herself):*
> Cocoa butter.

LES *(unable to leave the subject alone):*
> Promise me, Trace. Promise me if you find out you'll tell.

TRACY:
> Relax, Les. Lighten up. *(Beat)* Wouldn't my old lady have a bird if somebody wrote something like that about her on a washroom wall? Wouldn't that be a scream?

LES *(addressing* **FINESTAD***):*
> It's all over the change stalls in Magic Marker. Every morning. You can't hardly get it off with Comet. Pictures too.

TRACY:
> The old cow immortalized on the wall of a can. "Edna Tolbertson, world famous organ grinder." She'd have a stroke! *To the tune of "Koolaid, Koolaid, tastes great" she sings:*
> "Edna say, 'Poontang, poontang, real great, / Poontang, poontang, can't wait!'" *(Beat)* See! *(She winks and exits laughing. Suddenly she holds the cigarettes aloft, brandishes them)*
> Puffers, kids!

I Had a Job I Liked. Once.

LES (*in a daze*):

> It's hard to believe. It's hard to believe that some people haven't got nothing better to do than torment and torture other people. It's hard to believe . . .

FINESTAD:

> Les!

LES (*his mind somewhere else*):

> What?

FINESTAD (*gently*):

> Come and sit down.

LES, *moving as if in a trance, takes his chair again.* **FINESTAD** *offers him a cigarette which* **LES** *accepts.* **FINESTAD** *takes one himself and lights* **LES'S,** *then his own.*

FINESTAD:

> Why'd you let Tracy Tolbertson mooch cigarettes, Les?

LES *shrugs.*

FINESTAD:

> Because she's pretty? (*Pause*) Because she was nice to you? (*Reflecting*) It's odd isn't it? How the things people want to tell and *don't* want to tell—are often the same things. Like your story about the writing on the walls.

LES (*suspiciously*):

> What the hell's that supposed to mean?

FINESTAD:

> You opened the door a crack and then you got scared, you tried to close it. But when I didn't let you—I believe you were thankful.

LES:

> You get your head any further up your ass you're going to suffocate.

FINESTAD:
> Let me lay it on the table for you. Heasman *believes* you're guilty because Tolbertson *wants* you to be. I'm the odd man out because I want everything done by the book. Now you ought to be able to figure this much out—that you're better off with me than them. Do you understand what I'm telling you, Les?

FINESTAD *waits for a reply, none comes.*

FINESTAD:
> Everything that crosses my desk, every case, I reason through step by step, according to Hoyle. I'm doing that on this case too. But once every ten years I permit myself a hunch. You're this decade's hunch, Les.

LES:
> Why?

FINESTAD *(pointing to the hallway):*
> When Tracy Tolbertson and her father were sitting out there, waiting to see me, I snuck a peek at her. She looked awful scared—scared of her old man.

LES *doesn't speak.*

FINESTAD:
> I need the truth to help you, Les. Don't hold out, son.

LES *staring hard, trying to make up his mind whether he can trust* **FINESTAD. FINESTAD** *proffers his hand halfway across the desk to be shaken.* **LES** *is uncertain whether to accept it or not.*

FINESTAD:
> Let's shake on it, Les. Let's shake on the truth.

LES *draws back in his chair, seems to shrink from taking the hand.*

FINESTAD *(leaning forward across the desk a little more):*
> Take it, son. Hand to a drowning man.

LES *stares, rubs his nose, twitches indecisively.*

FINESTAD *(louder, more insistent, reaching out a little farther):*
Take it!

LES *(plaintive):*
Jesus!

FINESTAD *(suddenly lunging forward across the desk as if to force him to accept it):*
Take it, goddamn it!

FINESTAD'S *awkward position, leaning out precariously over the desk, suddenly causes his back to knot. His face contorts, he lurches and staggers sideways, spilling papers from his desk to the floor.* **LES** *stands, alarmed. It looks to him like something very serious, perhaps a heart attack. He takes several steps backward, aghast.* **FINESTAD** *staggers to the blackboard where he props himself up, panting. It is obvious he is in acute pain.*

LES:
Is it your heart? *(He turns to the door, opens it, is about to call out)*

FINESTAD:
Wait! **(LES** *is halted by his tone.* **FINESTAD** *continues more quietly)* It's my back. *(He gestures helplessly)* My goddamn back goes out on me . . .

LES:
But shouldn't I call—

FINESTAD *(desperately):*
No! Don't call anyone! I can't let them see me like this.

LES:
But . . .

FINESTAD:
They'd laugh. *(Begging)* Please, son. Don't let them see me like this. Please don't give me away.

LES *stares at him.*

FINESTAD *(stretching his arms out to him):*
   Pull me right, Les.

LES:
   What?

FINESTAD:
   One good jerk on my wrists and I click back into place. My
   wife does it all the time.

LES *appears doubtful.*

FINESTAD *(speaking with difficulty because of the pain he is in):*
   I've got nobody else, Les. *(Pause)* Don't give me away to
   them. *(He reaches out again to* LES, *gasps with pain, holds his
   arms extended, waiting)* Les, it's bad.

It is apparent from LES'S *face that this appeal has moved him. Uncertain he is doing the right thing, he nevertheless closes the door. Then, impulsively, he steps forward and seizes* FINESTAD'S *wrists. The two of
them look into each other's eyes. Something passes between them.*
FINESTAD *collects himself, adopts a no-nonsense manner.*

FINESTAD:
   Let me brace myself. *(He spreads his legs to shoulder width,
   edges them backward gingerly)* On the count of three I want
   you to give me one hell of a pull. Don't be afraid. Ready?
   Okay. One, two, three! *(*LES *tugs diffidently, increasing*
   FINESTAD'S *pain)* No, no, suffering Mary and Joseph! A
   stiff one I said! Now again! One, two, three!

LES *heaves harder, but not hard enough.* FINESTAD *groans horribly.*
LES, *frightened, releases* FINESTAD'S *wrists.*

LES:
   I can't.

FINESTAD *(desperate):*
> The hell you can't! Take my wrists! Goddamn it, take them!

LES, *overawed by* **FINESTAD'S** *fierceness, does as he is told.*

FINESTAD:
> All right. One more time. You can do it, Les. Don't fail me.
> One, two, three!

This time **LES** *rears back ferociously and snaps* **FINESTAD** *hard.*

LES *(defiant):*
> Hard enough? Satisfied?

FINESTAD *straightens himself gingerly, cautiously. Finally fully
erect he stiffly circles* **LES,** *once, twice. The second time around he
moves more easily. Having completed his second circuit around the boy
he halts, smiles shyly.* **FINESTAD,** *slightly embarrassed by what has
transpired, moves off awkwardly, beginning to explain.*

FINESTAD:
> Irene says it's stress. I say sitting. Twenty years with your
> ass planted in a patrol car or behind a desk—it can bugger
> your back every bit as bad as lifting.

LES:
> Lift with your legs—then you'll wear. That's what my old
> man says.

FINESTAD *nods, as if accepting the advice. He moves to the desk.*

FINESTAD:
> You mind if I have one of your Cokes?

LES:
> You paid for them.

FINESTAD *(carefully, with a slight emphasis):*
> You mind if I have one of your Cokes?

LES *(taken aback):*
> Help yourself.

FINESTAD *(opening the bottle, drinking):*
> All right, Les. *(Beat)* You helped straighten out my problem.
> Now how about you let me try straighten out yours?

Fade to blackout.

Scene Two

The lights come up on **FINESTAD** *and* **LES** *seated in the office.*
FINESTAD *leans back in his chair listening to* **LES** *with marked atten-*
tion, smoking. There is an obvious change in LES'S attitude. Most of
the hostility to **FINESTAD** *has disappeared, although it is capable of re-*
surfacing in a flash. His manner is intense and earnest, a struggle to
convey what he thinks and feels.

LES:
> It only came to me this summer, you know? That I was in-
> visible. *(Laughs)* I mean, fuck, I thought I was flesh and
> blood and solid but certain people, certain *kinds* of people,
> were looking right through me. Not all people, like my old
> man sure as hell sees me because who else is he fucking yell-
> ing at? And Mike, he sees me, and the girls who have to
> work at the Dog 'N Suds, and the old ladies who shop at the
> Saan Store—these kind of people can see me. But the other
> kind—the ones that live in the nice houses, the ones that
> drive the Chrysler New Yorkers and Buick LeSabres, you
> know, the ones who sit on the Recreation Board, the fat old
> farts who waddle around the golf course and tip you a fuck-
> ing dime for hauling their golf bags around after them for
> three-and-a-half hours when you're thirteen years old, and
> blame you because they hit a duck hook, you were sup-
> posed to've moved or something—they look right through
> you, to them you're invisible. *(Pause)* And their kids too. To
> their kids you're invisible. *(Pause)* Like Tracy and her crowd
> at the pool. I stood right up to the grill but they never saw
> me. Didn't have a clue I was there. *(Pause)* I studied them.

Jesus, I even knew whose beach towel was whose. I spot an empty beach towel and I knew who'd jumped in the pool. The girls—they never swim—they just jump in when they get too hot from tanning. And the transistors going all the time, full blast. When the pumps are shut down I hear the music. Afternoons they always listen to Regina because during the day reception from Winnipeg is not so hot, but if they come back to the pool at night, they play Winnipeg because you can pick it up better at night and they got lots better disc jockeys on Winnipeg. *(Pause)* Nights they had parties. Teen parties, I mean. Somebody would bring a barbecue to do hamburgers and hot dogs. And there'd be a portable record player for dancing. *(Speaking quickly).* All the floodlights shining down and the underwater lights in the pool turning the water a beautiful green and the sky pitch black, or sometimes a big yellow moon, and everybody dancing in their bathing suits. *(Beat)* I used to sit in the dark and watch them. Soon as the party started I'd turn the lights out in the pump room. If I'd have had a light on they could have seen me watching at the window, right? So I sat in the dark. I held my cigarette like this. *(He holds up a cupped hand)* So they couldn't see the tip burning red in the window. My old man said that's the way they did it in the war, so they didn't give themselves away to the enemy. *(Beat)* They didn't even know I existed.

FINESTAD:
> Somebody did, Les.

LES:
> Who?

FINESTAD:
> Whoever wrote on the walls.

LES'S *distress is obvious. He shakes his head as if to deny it.*

FINESTAD *(speaking softly, sympathetically):*
> And every morning you came to work it was there and you had to scrub it off again.

LES *(in a whisper):*
Yeah.

FINESTAD:
Fill in that part of the story for me, Les. Patch that hole.
(Pause) Fill it in, Les. Tell me.

LES *gets to his feet, begins to pace in great agitation. He passes the blackboard and picks up the eraser, laughs, holding it up for* **FINESTAD** *to see:*

Every morning. Les and his trusty scrubbing brush. Heading for the crappers. *(A change comes over* **LES**. *He adopts the same attitude he did in the earlier flashback. He is in the past, although able to communicate with* **FINESTAD**. *The lights alter, creating a new location.* **LES** *moves in a reluctant manner, as if he were dragging a ball and chain, the arm that holds the blackboard eraser hanging as if it bears a great weight. He comes to a halt, turns to face the audience revealing that his eyes are screwed tightly shut, his face twisted like a wishing child's. He lifts both hands to shoulder height, revealing crossed fingers.* **FINESTAD** *looks on)*

LES:
Please. Please, please, please. Please give me a break this morning. *(Heartfelt)* Surprise me. *(He opens his eyes, half-turns and immediately his shoulders slump and his face falls. He stares and says in a monotone)* Six nights in a row. Don't they get tired? *(Pause)* I get tired. *(His arm slowly comes up, he points)* That one's old, they used that one already. *(Graffiti in different taped voices)* "Banging on Jilly, banging hard and strong / Who we going to bang on, when Jilly's dead and gone?" *(His arm drops and he shuffles around to face left. The arm rises as before and points)* Now this is new. "Star light, star bright / First star I see tonight / I wish I may, I wish I might / Have that old dilly, Jilly, play my skin flute tonight." *(Shuffles ninety degrees, presenting his back to the audience. Trembling arm lifts again, points)* "Jilly's ringadangdoo / What is that? / Soft and furry like a pussy cat." *(He shuffles ninety degrees to the right)* "Buffalo gal won't you come out

44

tonight. Come out tonight—" *(Unable to continue he covers his ears with his hands, stands, apparently frozen. After a time his hands fall to his sides, the audience glimpses his strained, rigid profile. Suddenly he attacks the graffiti with the eraser, scrubbing desperately to obliterate what he sees there)*

FINESTAD *(rising in alarm):*
    Les!

LES *continues as if possessed. His work becomes increasingly wild. He sweeps the brush in great, frantic arcs.*

FINESTAD *(moving around his desk):*
    Les!

LES *moves to another imaginary wall. He is like a wild animal, trapped, throwing itself against the bars of its cage.*

FINESTAD:
    Stop it, Les! Goddamn it, stop!

LES *turns to face the audience.* **FINESTAD** *seizes his shoulders from behind, shakes him.*

FINESTAD:
    That's enough, Les! Enough!

LES *looks at him with a wild, haunted expression.*

FINESTAD:
    No more, Les!

FINESTAD *takes* **LES** *by the elbow, begins to guide him back to his chair:*
    Take it easy, son. It's okay.

The boy abruptly wrenches himself out of **FINESTAD'S** *grasp in a sudden explosive movement. It is a demonstration that he isn't weak, that he is capable of standing alone.*

LES *(blurting it out, on the verge of tears):*
Fuckers. They thought they got it cheap! They paid!

FINESTAD:
Got what cheap, Les?

LES:
Cheap bunkers. Cheap traps. Couple of those guys must have welded their back teeth together when they hit that with a sand wedge.

FINESTAD:
Hit what?

LES:
Cinder blocks. Night came I took them off the construction site for the clubhouse addition. Heavy as lead—I packed some half a mile or more in the dark and me fourteen, small for my age too. Buried them in the sand traps, just below the surface. *(He demonstrates with a golf swing)* Whack! Tear your clubhead off you hit that! Tear your asshole loose you hit that! *(Pause)* If you're going to be invisible, that's the way to be it. Like that. *(He smacks his fist into his palm as he pronounces each word)* Like . . . a . . . fucking . . . cinder . . . block.

FINESTAD:
All right, Les. *(Coaxing)* You got it out. Take a chair.

LES *stays where he is.*

FINESTAD *(beckoning, shifting the chair invitingly):*
It's okay, Les. Come.

The door flies open and a flustered **HEASMAN** *abruptly enters.*

HEASMAN:
We got trouble.

FINESTAD:
What kind of trouble?

HEASMAN:
>Tolbertson's outside. He's demanding to see you—won't take no for an answer. They're trying to hold him at the desk so's I can warn you.

FINESTAD:
>All right. We don't want him barging in here with the boy in the office. Get him out of sight.

HEASMAN *(rattled):*
>Where out of sight?

FINESTAD:
>For Christ's sake, Heasman, where do you think? The base-ment. Take him down to the basement. They aren't going to cross paths in the basement, are they?

TOLBERTSON *(off):*
>I know perfectly well where I'm going! I don't need an es-cort thank you! *He barges in the door and comes face to face with* **LES** *and* **HEASMAN**. *A moment of extreme tension. Anything could happen.*

FINESTAD *(gesturing to Les):*
>Go with Corporal Heasman. Now.

HEASMAN *takes the boy by the arm and hurries him out.*
TOLBERTSON *watches them go, then swings around and confronts*
FINESTAD. TOLBERTSON *is dressed in a white shirt, tieless and unbuttoned at the collar. He is wearing a dark blue suit, the jacket hanging open. He fights to control his distaste for* **FINESTAD**.

TOLBERTSON *(grimly):*
>Sergeant Finestad.

FINESTAD *(indicating the chair):*
>Won't you have a seat?

TOLBERTSON:
>I don't intend to be put off any longer. What are you

doing about this matter concerning my daughter?

FINESTAD:
One of my men was supposed to tell you that I would call in the morning and fill you in completely. You did get the message, didn't you?

TOLBERTSON:
I decided not to wait. Has the charge been laid?

FINESTAD:
No charge has been laid. The matter remains under investigation.

TOLBERTSON *(derisively)*:
Under investigation! You're telling me that he's been in custody all this time and he's still denying it?

FINESTAD:
I haven't raised the question of guilt yet. He can't be expected to deny an accusation that hasn't been put to him.

TOLBERTSON *moves to the hard chair in front of the desk and grips the back with both hands.*

TOLBERTSON *(struggling to master himself)*:
Sergeant Finestad, I am not, by nature, a patient man. But if an apology is required to get action—I will make it. You are a proud man. Perhaps the premium I have placed on efficiency, on results, has made you feel that I rode roughshod over you, that I did not show you the respect you deserve. If that was the impression I left with you, forgive me. *(Pause)* But let me assure you that our goal was always the same, regardless of our differences in approach. What we both sought was justice.

FINESTAD:
No. Not justice.

TOLBERTSON *(surprised)*:
>   Pardon me?

FINESTAD:
>   I gave up on justice long ago. It's a mystery to me. I have no
>   idea what it is. I stick with law. It's safer than justice.

TOLBERTSON *(trying to interrupt)*:
>   Sergeant Finestad . . .

FINESTAD *(indicating the statute book)*:
>   Look, here it is. Black and white. This I can put my finger
>   on. What's justice? An idea rattling loose in our heads,
>   different to each of us. Which in the end means justice boils
>   down to what *I* think, what *I* believe, what *I want.* So when
>   anyone throws that word around I get nervous. Because
>   what they're really pushing is themselves. The rules,
>   however, remain the rules.

TOLBERTSON *(impatiently)*:
>   These schoolboy debates don't interest me. Let's get to the
>   point. What do you intend to do about this boy—

FINESTAD *(interrupting)*:
>   It is the point.

TOLBERTSON:
>   What? Your precious rules? Behaving as if you were a robot?

FINESTAD:
>   Why not? A robot can't recognize the colour of anybody's
>   skin, or guess his politics, or estimate the thickness of his
>   wallet. Maybe that's the kind of cops we need—

TOLBERTSON *(interrupting)*:
>   I don't find these speculations of yours amusing, Finestad.
>   If you want to parade your obsessions, do it someplace else,
>   some other time. *(Pointing to the book)* You cling to that the
>   way a child clings to a teddy bear. Security I suppose. But
>   against what?

FINESTAD:
Perhaps men without principles.

TOLBERTSON:
Meaning me?

FINESTAD:
You can answer that question with more certainty than I.

TOLBERTSON:
Self-righteousness is the least becoming of traits. Your men laugh at you, do you realize that?

FINESTAD:
And admire you. More's the pity.

TOLBERTSON *(coldly threatening):*
If I were you, I'd be careful.

FINESTAD:
That time's passed.

TOLBERTSON:
Which means what? Filing a complaint against me? Something specific?

FINESTAD:
No, nothing specific. I never suggested you were careless. Just without principles.

TOLBERTSON:
If you don't have a complaint, perhaps I do. *(Pause)* But for the time being let's leave my complaint in the realm of theory. Tonight a question has arisen. What's behind the eccentric way you're behaving?

FINESTAD:
You tell me.

TOLBERTSON:

Two possible explanations. The one most flattering to you is that you believe my daughter is lying. *(Pause)* She is not. *(Pause)* The second and more likely is that you see this as an opportunity to punish me. If this complaint—which I hasten to say is still a theoretical one—reached the ears of your superiors as well as the office of the Attorney General, it would be listened to. Particularly given your current unpopularity with your men. **(TOLBERTSON** *allows this to sink in, then continues)* The least the Crown can expect from the police is cooperation in handling cases. In the past, your cooperation has been tendered most grudgingly. But in this instance, if cooperation is refused for the most obvious, petty, and personal of motives, then action would have to be taken.

TOLBERTSON *waits for* **FINESTAD** *to reply.* **FINESTAD** *remains silent.*

TOLBERTSON:

I repeat. This complaint is still a theoretical one. It does not have to be made. Do you understand me?

FINESTAD:

I understand you.

TOLBERTSON *(feeling he is in the driver's seat):*

Well then. Let's review your progress—or lack of it— in the case so far.

FINESTAD:

If you insist.

TOLBERTSON *(unconsciously assuming the pose of a cross-examining attorney):*

So you haven't actually asked this boy whether he did it or not. Is that correct?

FINESTAD:

Correct.

TOLBERTSON:
Why?

FINESTAD:
The time wasn't right.

TOLBERTSON:
Not right? Have you taken any sort of statement from the suspect?

FINESTAD:
No.

TOLBERTSON *(sarcastically)*:
Curious. *(Beat)* Why?

FINESTAD:
I expect the boy will make a complete statement when we come to the end of the questioning.

TOLBERTSON:
A hopeful attitude.

FINESTAD:
Based on experience.

TOLBERTSON *(mockingly)*:
Experience.

FINESTAD:
That's what I said.

TOLBERTSON:
It appears that so far you have exerted yourself very little in this case, Sergeant Finestad. Is it too much to ask whether you have troubled to exert yourself to the extent of actually reading the complaint?

FINESTAD:
I have read the complaint.

TOLBERTSON:
> Carefully?

FINESTAD:
> Very carefully.

TOLBERTSON:
> Then you know what I want.

FINESTAD:
> Mr. Tolbertson, nobody always gets what he wants.

TOLBERTSON:
> He's a pig.

FINESTAD *shrugs.*

TOLBERTSON:
> A pig raised by a pig. The old sow's a drunk and a whore.

FINESTAD *is impassive.*

TOLBERTSON:
> I want him charged.

FINESTAD *(flatly):*
> The decision whether or not to lay a charge will be made
> after I have reviewed all the evidence. Not before.

TOLBERTSON *says accusingly in a hushed voice:*
> You son of a bitch. You weren't there tonight. You didn't
> find what my wife and I found.

FINESTAD:
> No, I didn't.

TOLBERTSON *(struggling with his emotion):*
> My little girl—*(Giving way)* Goddamn it, she was
> half-naked!

FINESTAD:
> Yes.

TOLBERTSON:
> Explain that to me! Explain to me how she came to be naked from the waist down!

FINESTAD:
> I don't know. It may have been her choice.

TOLBERTSON *makes a move towards* **FINESTAD** *that suggests he is on the brink of attacking him.* **FINESTAD** *stops him with a look.*

FINESTAD:
> No. You don't want that. Not with me.

TOLBERTSON *swings away violently, stands for several seconds struggling to master his feelings. When he has achieved a tenuous control of them he slowly turns around to face* **FINESTAD.**

TOLBERTSON *(shakily):*
> You . . . you have the *gall* to tell me that what I saw tonight isn't sufficient evidence for laying a charge?

FINESTAD:
> Sufficient evidence to prompt an investigation. Not for a charge.

TOLBERTSON:
> Good God, if you could have seen her . . . cowering, huddled up against the back wall of the garage. Trying to hide, like an animal *(wonderingly)* caught in the headlights of the car when we drove in. *(Momentarily losing his voice, then recovering it)* When he tried to do that . . . She lost her key to the house. Couldn't get inside to phone anyone for help. Couldn't go to the neighbours the way she was . . . Nothing to do but creep in there, in the garage, wait, *hide* until we got home. *(Lost in his explanation)* You see that, don't you? That it was all she could do?

TOLBERTSON'S *obvious and sincere pain has its effect on*
FINESTAD. *For the first time he appears somewhat shaken.*

FINESTAD:
> It's been a very long night, a very hard and trying night.
> Please sit down.

TOLBERTSON *(blindly shaking his head):*
> I don't want to sit.

FINESTAD *(pleading):*
> Then go home and get some rest. Go home to your wife.
> She'll be worried.

TOLBERTSON:
> Worried? No, that isn't the word for my wife. Hysterical is a
> more accurate description of Edna at present. True, it was a
> terrible shock. But for her to act as if somehow I'm to blame.
> As if it's all my fault. *(Pause, gathers himself)* If you had seen
> my daughter—you wouldn't have any doubts. Not if you'd
> seen her.

FINESTAD *(gently, sympathetically):*
> And maybe if you'd seen the boy, talked to him as I have,
> maybe you would.

TOLBERTSON:
> All those cases—it wasn't just winning. I never went after
> anybody I didn't *know* was guilty. I had to know it. *Know* it.
> And when I knew it, the guilty ones never walked if I could
> help it. *(Pause)* Grant did it. That I know.

FINESTAD:
> If he did, I promise you I'll get to the bottom of it.

TOLBERTSON *(dully):*
> If I'd have caught him there I'd have killed him. *(He looks at*
> **FINESTAD***)* This isn't bragging. *(He finally sits, looks at his*
> *hands)* If the law is meant to settle accounts—it doesn't offer
> enough to settle this one. Not for this.

FINESTAD *(quietly):*
> Go home.

TOLBERTSON *(looking around him, as if his surroundings suddenly strike him as strange):*
> Yes. Home. *(He slowly gets to his feet)* My daughter expects things of me. She takes it as a matter of course that I do not lose to the likes of Les Grant. *(Hesitates)* My wife objects to my influence on my daughter, that I speak my mind, express certain opinions. My wife calls me callous, hard. She says young girls should not be exposed to these things—my wife believes girls were made to dream, embrace certain illusions. *(Shakes his head)* But the world is what it is. Isn't it? *(Pause)* No matter how hard I was, I was never hard enough to prepare her for this.

FINESTAD:
> Go home.

TOLBERTSON:
> Of course. *(He pats his pockets, searching for car keys. He looks suddenly aged, slightly bewildered. He locates the keys, looks at them lying in the palm of his hand)* You know me, Finestad.

FINESTAD:
> Yes.

TOLBERTSON:
> This is not meant as a threat. Threats do not seem to have any effect on you. It is only a statement of fact. You know I make a bad enemy. Charge him or you will regret it. I will go to any length, *any length*, to see he gets what he deserves.

FINESTAD:
> So will I.

TOLBERTSON:
> You may hate me but it's not just between the two of us.

I Had a Job I Liked. Once.

FINESTAD:
> It's not about hating you—

TOLBERTSON (*interrupting*):
> It's about my daughter too. Think of my daughter the way she was at eleven o'clock tonight. Think of her.

FINESTAD:
> I am sorry for your daughter. I am sorry for your wife. I am even sorry for you, Tolbertson.

TOLBERTSON:
> But?

FINESTAD:
> No buts. Just sorry.

TOLBERTSON:
> Then I had better be off. (**TOLBERTSON** *begins to absent-mindedly button up his suit jacket. His fingers linger on the last button*) There is a frost warning out tonight for low-lying areas. I heard it on the radio earlier, driving here.

When **FINESTAD** *doesn't respond* **TOLBERTSON** *begins to move off towards the door. Halfway there he stops and turns around.*

TOLBERTSON:
> She's just seventeen. Think of that. Imagine what you'd do if you had a child . . .

TOLBERTSON *exits.*

When the door closes **FINESTAD** *is obviously disconcerted. He appears to be weighing what he has heard. Suddenly the words* **NOT PERSONAL** *catch his eye. He strides abruptly to the blackboard, erases them angrily, marches to the door, yanks it open and begins to shout into the corridor.*

FINESTAD:
> Heasman! Heasman! Somebody get Heasman and Grant in
> my office! Now!

FINESTAD *turns, seizes the statute book and slams it on the desk.
There is a new look on his face, determined, stony. The lights slowly
fade out on that look.*

Blackout.

ACT TWO

FINESTAD *and* **LES** *are seated at the desk as before.* **FINESTAD'S** *manner is more severe, more professional than previously. The change has its effect on* **LES,** *making him slightly uneasy.*

FINESTAD:
>I think it is safe to say that we've passed through the preliminaries now, the little dance of getting to know one another. We do know one another a bit now, wouldn't you say?

LES *(grudgingly):*
>Suppose so.

FINESTAD:
>Good. *(Beat)* The time has come for me to put some of the hard questions to you. Questions that matter. You must answer them truthfully, hiding nothing. If you lie, or tell half-truths, it will worsen your case. Do you understand what I am saying?

LES *nods.*

FINESTAD:
>I'm not so foolish as to pretend that what happened earlier tonight has made us friends. If I did that you would suspect me of playing a cheap and stupid trick. You would be right. We are not friends. But we understand each other. You know I have been straight with you. Will you be straight with me?

LES:
>Yeah . . . all right.

FINESTAD:
> Good. Then shall we begin?

LES *nods uneasily.*

FINESTAD:
> While you and Corporal Heasman were in the basement
> Mr. Tolbertson and I had an interesting conversation. I
> learned something from it.

LES:
> Yeah?

FINESTAD:
> Tolbertson is really convinced you did it.

LES *fails to react.*

FINESTAD:
> Maybe I was blind, Les. At first it was principles that kept
> me from giving in to him. And then after talking to you for
> a while, I started to believe you weren't capable of what
> they claimed. Was that bad judgement on my part?

LES *doesn't respond.*

FINESTAD:
> Les, were you and Tracy going out together, seeing each
> other without her father knowing?

LES *still doesn't reply.*

FINESTAD *(hopeful that his theory is true):*
> You both knew how her father would feel about her dating
> you. So your meetings were on the sly. *(Beat)* Tonight no dif-
> ferent than any other night.

LES:
> No way.

FINESTAD *(boring in):*

> You're hiding something, Les.

LES:

> Me? What am I hiding?

FINESTAD:

> Whatever went wrong in the car tonight. *(Beat)* Could be
> things went further than she meant them to. It happens.
> Could be she got upset, hysterical even, jumped out of your
> car before she realized what she was doing. *(Pause)* Seeing
> her, could be you panicked, beat it. Stranding her. *(Pause)*
> And when her father discovered her like that—she needed
> answers, fast.

LES:

> Dream on dreamer.

FINESTAD:

> You're protecting her, Les.

LES:

> Give me a break.

FINESTAD:

> What you're doing, Les, isn't chivalrous. It's only stupid.
> This isn't like providing her with cigarettes so Daddy
> doesn't find out and blow his top. This is serious.

LES:

> Okay, okay, so I had the hots for Tracy Tolbertson. Is that a
> joke? I knew I wasn't Bob Marsh with my own car and the
> right clothes and all the time in the world to lay around the
> pool turning myself into a Coppertoned asshole. I wasn't in
> that league. Tracy Tolbertson doesn't go out with geeks like
> me. She'd rather shave her dog and take it to a school dance
> than go with somebody pathetic like me. *(Lying)* I wasn't
> dumb enough to think it was romance. But I thought maybe
> it was like friends, you know? Do you maybe understand
> that? Huh?

FINESTAD:

Yes. *(Pause)* I made a mistake.

LES:

Well, so did I. So did I.

FINESTAD *and* **LES** *remain silent for a time.*

FINESTAD:

I thought because she was in your car tonight . . . I read something into it.

LES:

You ought to get your reading glasses changed.

FINESTAD *(after a long pause):*

Then is Tolbertson right, Les? Did you try to rape his daughter tonight?

LES *takes considerable time before answering. He looks directly into* **FINESTAD'S** *eyes during this interval. When he answers he does so with great conviction.*

LES:

No, I did not try to rape his daughter. No way.

FINESTAD:

Then you had better tell me, tell me *exactly* what happened tonight. From beginning to end.

LES:

Beginning to end?

FINESTAD:

I need to know, Les.

LES, *rising from his chair and beginning to prowl about the office with suppressed energy, snatches up the two hard-backed chairs in front of* **FINESTAD'S** *desk, carries them some distance off and plunks them down, begins to arrange them side by side to represent the front seat of a*

*car. As he does this he begins his story. When he seats himself, pop
music from the sixties comes up softly under his voice. As in previous
flashbacks* **FINESTAD** *remains, for the time being, behind his desk, dis-
tant, but an intent observer and sometime participant in the story.*

LES:

I had the old man's car tonight—make a mark on the wall.
He said I could take it as long as I brought it back with a full
tank. I checked when I took it—it was half full, but that's
the old man all over again. So fucking tight he squeaks
when he walks. Anyway, I finished work as per usual, it
was about nine-thirty before I got the machinery put to bed
and the pool locked up tighter than a nun's . . . excuse my
English, I forgot you're Catholic. Anyway, I was just tooling
around town with the radio playing and the windows
rolled down, trying to blow the stink of chlorine off me . . . I
always smell of it, you know, the Javex smell—

FINESTAD *(interrupting):*

You're alone now. Tracy isn't with you?

LES:

I'm coming to that.

FINESTAD:

Pardon.

LES:

So I'm cruising, as I said. When who do I see but Tracy
Tolbertson hammering on down the sidewalk like she was
going to a fire. So I thought to myself, Now she looks like she
could use a ride. So I pulled over and offered, you know?

*A change in lighting should suggest a soft summer night, the light dim
and uncertain.* **LES** *pulls the car over and switches off the radio. The
music ceases. He leans across the front seat and opens the door to the
passenger side of the car.*

LES:

Tracy! Hey, Trace!

TRACY *enters wearing sandals, skirt and halter top. She pauses, trying to make out the car and its driver, then approaches hesitantly, not sure who it is calling to her.*

LES:
> It's me, Trace!

TRACY *pokes her head into the opened door, finally recognizing* **LES.**

TRACY:
> Oh, it's you. I didn't know who it was at first.

LES:
> Yeah, well it's me. Can I give you a ride somewheres?

TRACY *(looking around the inside of the car):*
> I didn't know you had a car, Les. When did you buy this old reservation beater? *(Ironically)* Nice wheels.

LES *(embarrassed and stiff):*
> It's the old man's.

TRACY *(laughing):*
> Oops. Apologies to the head of the household.

LES *(trying to make light of the situation):*
> So can I give you a lift anywheres in my junker?

TRACY *(looking back in the direction from where she came):*
> I don't think so, Les.

LES *(insistent):*
> It looked to me like you were going somewhere in a hurry. Really stepping out. Even this rust bucket's faster if you're in a hurry.

LES *waits for an answer while* **TRACY,** *silent, gazes back over her shoulder.*

I Had a Job I Liked. Once.

LES:
> So what do you say?

TRACY (*making up her mind*):
> All right.

She hops in, settles herself on the seat.

LES (*touching the brim of an imaginary chauffeur's cap*):
> James at your service, ma'am. Where to?

TRACY:
> The Dog 'N Suds. (*Sharply*) No, not there. Oh, I don't know.
> Anywhere. Just drive.

LES:
> Done.

LES *draws the car away from the curb. He drives while* **TRACY** *sits stonily beside him. He casts quick glances her way, trying to gauge her mood.*

LES:
> If you smell anything funny—well don't think it's me, eh?
> The old man forgot his lunch—a sardine sandwich—in the
> glove compartment last weekend. Sardine seems to have
> killed the air freshener. (*Laughs nervously*) I got one dead
> pine tree in this car, I guess.

TRACY *smiles condescendingly.*

LES:
> You want the radio? I can get Winnipeg. The car's a piece of
> junk but the radio's pretty good. You want the radio on?

LES *reaches out to switch the radio on.*

TRACY (*in an expressionless but commanding voice*):
> Leave it off.

LES:

> Sure. Sure thing, Tracy.

They drive on for a while, **LES** *repeatedly rubbing his nose and throwing darting, furtive looks her way.*

LES:

> You thinking, Tracy? Because if you're thinking I don't want to interrupt. *(Lamely)* If you're thinking.

TRACY:

> Bob and I just had a fight.

LES *(unable to disguise his delight):*

> Who? You and Bob Marsh? Bob the Bog?

TRACY:

> We broke up. After only a month of going steady. I can't seem to make a go of anything with a guy.

LES:

> Well . . . with him maybe. But really, he's a grade A dork. Who could? I mean make a go of it. With him.

TRACY *(turning to* **LES***):*

> He makes me so mad sometimes! He's the most selfish, inconsiderate person—Tonight there's this party—probably the last party of the summer—and I asked him:
>
> Could he please get me a bottle of crème de menthe for the party? I love crème de menthe. And so he forgets or something, he was out golfing with his father, some lame excuse, and he claims it was too late for him to find somebody to pull him a bottle before the Liquor Board closed. And so we had this big fight and I told him what I thought of him and now I guess I get to miss the party. *(Pause)* So what do you think of that?

LES *(shakes his head):*

> Pretty shitty.

TRACY *(settling back with her arms hugging her breasts):*
> So if I seem moody and unsociable, you know the reason why.

Keeping silent they drive on for a time.

LES *(summoning up his courage):*
> Tracy?

TRACY:
> What?

LES:
> I was thinking—maybe you don't have to miss the party. *(Hurrying on as if in fear of being stopped)* I could go to the poolroom and pay somebody to pull us a case of beer from off-sale. I know it's not crème de menthe but it's booze, right? So if the two of us went to this party, like together, we'd have something to drink and it wouldn't be so bad and you might have a pretty decent time anyway.

TRACY *(appalled by this suggestion):*
> No . . . no, I don't think so, Les.

LES *(excited by his proposal):*
> If you're afraid that Bob maybe'll kick up a fuss or something like that—

TRACY:
> It's not that, Les.

LES *(brought up short):*
> What then?

TRACY:
> Well, the party's private kind of. Invitations only. So it would be . . . *awkward.*

LES:
> Like I would be about as popular as syphilis is what you're saying.

TRACY:
> I said awkward. Don't put words in my mouth.

Both stare straight ahead, tight-lipped, tense.

LES:
> What's wrong with me, Tracy?

TRACY:
> What are you talking about?

LES *(passionately):*
> I'm talking about the pool, about the things that people write on the changeroom walls. Things they write about my mother, knowing it's me that has to clean them up.

TRACY *(staring out the side window):*
> People get bored. They like to stir things up a bit.

LES:
> Who's doing it, Tracy? Who's writing that stuff?

TRACY *(still looking out the window):*
> Search me.

LES:
> You're at the pool all day. You'd hear them laughing about it. Where's the joke if nobody knows who's doing it?

LES *waits for a reply. None comes.*

LES:
> I done you a lot of favours this summer, didn't I? Can't you do me this one? I got to know. It's driving me crazy. In the morning, before I go into those washrooms my stomach is upset, like before a big test—only worse, a lot worse.

TRACY:
> Speaking of bored, Les. Change the record, why don't you? (**TRACY** *turns away from the window to* **LES**) Read my lips.

(Slowly and carefully she enunciates) I . . . don't . . . know. *(Pause)* Is it sinking in?

LES:

If you'd just maybe even hint—

TRACY *(angrily interrupting):*

All right, that's it. Take me home. Here I'm having one of the worst nights of my life and you've suddenly got to start in on me with this crap which I've told you, I can't count how many times—at the pool even—that I don't know anything about and I don't *care* to know anything about, I'm not interested in who's writing on what walls what things and *still* you won't leave it alone.

LES:

I don't mean to upset you, Tracy. But don't you see? This business keeps going around in my head, it doesn't let up on me, I think about it all the time —

TRACY *(holding up her hand, speaking coldly and peremptorily):*
Not another word, Les.

LES *lapses into a restive silence.*

TRACY *(conciliatory):*

If you can be good company, if you can be nice, Les, you don't have to take me home. Can you do that?

LES *makes no reply.*

TRACY:

All right then, take me home. There's one thing I can't stand, it's a sulker.

LES:

I'm not sulking.

TRACY:

You are. You're acting like a big cry baby, feeling sorry for yourself. And who's the one who broke up tonight?

LES:
> You.

TRACY:
> You got it, mister. Me. Tracy broke up with somebody
> tonight.

LES:
> Consider yourself lucky.

TRACY:
> Well! As a matter of fact, I don't feel lucky! Maybe I cared
> for Bob Marsh.

LES:
> Why? I mean what is it with the guys I seen you going out
> with ever since maybe grade eight?

TRACY:
> This is my street! You can drop me right here! Last house on
> the end. *(Pointing)* That one right there, just stop the car.

LES *stops the car. Turns off the keys. Squints through the windshield at
the house.*

LES:
> I bet you got a fireplace in your house. *(Turns to* **TRACY***)*
> You got a fireplace in your house?

TRACY *(puzzled, bobs her head)*:
> Sure we have a fireplace.

LES *(looking at the house)*:
> I bet you got a rumpus room. You got a rumpus room in
> your house?

TRACY:
> Yes.

LES:
> I bet you Bob Marsh has a rumpus room and a fireplace his house. Am I right?

TRACY *nods.*

LES:
> And every boyfriend you've had since you were twelve years old—all those stupid horses' patoots I've seen you with—I bet you every one of them had a rumpus room and a fireplace their houses too.

TRACY:
> What if they did?

LES:
> And I bet they all have to have certain kinds of clothes, desert boots and like that. No pointy-toed black shoes. And tans. You ever went out with a guy who didn't have a pretty nice tan, Trace? Didn't look like one of the Beach Boys?

TRACY:
> You tell me. You seem to be the expert. Why you acting like this all of a sudden?

LES *(as if he doesn't hear her):*
> I work at a swimming pool and here I am, white as Caspar the Ghost. *(Beat)* Ever seen me at the grill watching one of your pool parties, Trace? Not likely.

TRACY:
> Get normal, Les.

LES:
> That's my summer right there, Trace. Dead white. You ever see skin so pale?

TRACY:
> Oh sure. Les'd *have* to be the whitest. Check me out, you

want to see fair skin. In a mirror, naked, I look like I'm wearing a white bikini.

LES *(to himself)*:
It's not the same, Tracy. Big difference.

TRACY:
Big difference! Look at that, big difference! *(She turns down the front of her skirt, exposing her belly)* There's white for you.

The way in which LES *looks at her naked belly awakens* TRACY *to what she has impulsively done. She reaches out and takes hold of his arm, presses it down on her abdomen, ostensibly for purposes of comparison.*

TRACY:
What'd I say? Every bit as white as you, aren't I?

LES *does not say a word. He stares down dumbly at his arm lying where it does.* TRACY *assumes he is rendered speechless by the position he finds himself in.*

TRACY:
What's the matter, Les? Cat got your tongue?

LES *(without lifting his head)*:
Who's doing it, Tracy? Who's writing that stuff about my mother on the changeroom walls?

TRACY:
Excuse me, but I'm out of here. *(She prepares to leave the car. As she does,* LES, *head still hanging, tucks his hand into the waistband of her skirt and prevents her from going.* TRACY, *horrified, protests)* Les! Les! What are you doing? Get your hand out of there, Les! *(Struggling)* Let me go! Let me go or I'll scream!

LES *(hanging on grimly, head still bowed)*:
So scream.

TRACY *(ceasing to fight, trying to imbue her voice with authority):*
I'm not telling you again, Les. I mean it.

LES:
Not until you tell me.

TRACY *(throwing a fit):*
You son of a bitch! Pervert! *(She claws and scratches his arm with a deliberate, furious intent to injure)* Let me go!

Scarcely flinching **LES** *submits to the attack until* **TRACY** *realizes it is pointless. She falls back, panting,* **LES** *still doggedly holding on.*

LES:
Finished?

TRACY:
Creep. Loser.

LES:
Who did it? Just tell me.

TRACY:
You really want to know? All the guys. Don. Bob. They didn't go for a piss they didn't take a pen along.

LES:
Why?

TRACY:
Because you're so pathetic, that's why. Trying to wiggle and worm your way in where you don't belong. That's loser stuff, Les. Begging to be liked. It's pathetic. Grow a spine.

LES *(stunned):*
And the girls' washroom . . . ?

TRACY *turns away, so as not to have to answer.*

LES:

The girls' washroom?

TRACY:

Who do you think?

LES *is so shocked he releases his grip on her waistband.* **TRACY** *notes this.*

TRACY:

You don't have any friends, so you don't understand how it is. They're my *friends*, Les. It was just a giggle.

LES *(shocked):*

Giggle?

TRACY:

A game. My old man and my old lady counting the china. *(Pause)* You and my mother, Les. Two peas in a pod.

LES:

What?

TRACY *(a confession):*

You're just like her. Maybe you and my mother think you're better than other people, but you're not. You're worse. Know why? Because you invite people to walk all over you like a door mat. Maybe Dad couldn't stop himself, even if he wanted to. *(Beat)* It's sick. You think I don't want to *like* my own mother?

LES:

That's nuts.

TRACY *(recovering her composure):*

Like my Dad says. There are two kinds of people in this world. People who get done to, people who do. My old lady gets done to. That's not for me!

LES:

It's my mother we're talking about—

TRACY:

Les, if you want to get even, go ahead, buy yourself a pen and write whatever you'd like about my mother. Do it!

LES *(with an edge of hysteria):*

You can say that when it isn't true! It's different when it's true!

TRACY:

If it's true, what are you complaining about? Anybody's entitled to say anything, as long as it's true. Ask my father, he's a lawyer.

LES *(growing more emotional):*

Don't you know anything about shame?

TRACY:

Now you sound like my mother.

LES:

Can't you guess what it feels like?

TRACY:

I don't want to guess! *(Pause. Trying to distance herself from him)* Really, Les. It's been a wonderful summer. Thanks for the loans, thanks for the cigarettes, most of all, thanks for the laughs. But I've got to be going.

LES:

I'm here, Tracy! Goddamn it, I'm here! Look at me!

TRACY *(frightened):*

Les—

LES:

You should know what it feels like.

TRACY:
> I'm going, Les.

LES *(seizing her waistband):*
> Maybe I ought to send you home in your white bikini tonight. That'd get around, too. Tracy's white bikini. That'd be as funny as any writing on a wall.

TRACY:
> Les!

LES:
> Tracy in her white bikini. (**LES** *gives a little tug to the waistband of her skirt)* Oops and they're off.

*As **LES** grows more agitated, **FINESTAD** rises from behind his desk and, concerned, begins to move towards the couple.*

TRACY:
> Les . . . don't act crazy.

LES:
> It's only fair, Trace. You said for me to get even. Let's do it! Let's get even.

TRACY:
> Les!

LES:
> Just so you know, Trace. Just so you know how it feels.

TRACY *(begging):*
> Please, Les. I . . .

LES:
> They got to come off, Trace.

TRACY:
> No.

LES:
> Yes.

TRACY:
> Let go!

LES:
> I'm somebody, Tracy! I ain't this summer's joke! Maybe you are!

TRACY *(overlapping):*
> Les!

FINESTAD *(in a commanding voice):*
> Les!

LES:
> They got to come off, Tracy.

FINESTAD:
> Les!

FINESTAD takes **TRACY** *by the shoulders and lifts her from the chair. She then exits.* **LES** *looks around dazed. Once more there is only* **FINESTAD** *and* **LES.**

FINESTAD:
> So you did it? You stripped her skirt and panties off?

LES:
> Fair's fair.

FINESTAD *(shaken):*
> Christ Almighty! What else did you do, Les?

LES:
> I didn't touch her—that way. I just threw the bitch and her little white ass out of my car.

TRACY *(off-stage, hysterical):*
> Let me in, Les! Somebody's going to come by! Please! Let me in!

LES:
> She wanted back in. She wouldn't have wanted back in if she thought I was going to rape her. Right?

TRACY *(off-stage):*
> Let me in, Les! Somebody's going to come by! Please! Let me in!

LES *(overlapping):*
> Get away from this car, Trace! Fuck off! No way I'm letting you back in!

TRACY:
> Les, please! Somebody's going to see me!

LES *(overlapping):*
> This is how it feels, Tracy! Now you know! Now you know!

FINESTAD *(overlapping):*
> Stop it! Stop it, Les! Now sit!

LES *sits.* **FINESTAD** *is furious with himself, furious with the boy.*

FINESTAD:
> You stupid little shit! What is wrong with you? What the fuck is wrong?

LES *doesn't reply, doesn't look at him.*

FINESTAD:
> You look at me when I'm talking to you! Look at me!

LES *lifts his eyes and stares at* **FINESTAD.** **FINESTAD** *collects himself, calms himself a little.*

FINESTAD:
> All right. All right then. God's truth now, Les. You didn't try to rape her?

LES *(monotone):*
> No.

FINESTAD:
> You pulled off her skirt and underpants and pushed her out of the car? That's all you did? It wasn't that she got away from you?

LES:
> If she got away why did she stand there begging me to unlock the door? If I was trying to rape her why did she ask me to open the door and let her back in the car? She was still standing there bare-assed when I peeled rubber, took off.

FINESTAD:
> What did you do with the clothes?

LES:
> I drove around for a while. And then I started to realize what I'd done. So I put the pedal to the metal, headed out of town, and let the wind blow them away.

FINESTAD *(exasperated):*
> Christ Almighty!

LES:
> All I wanted was to humiliate her like she done me. They can't say I tried to rape her.

FINESTAD:
> You goddamn right they can. *(Fiercely)* That's exactly what they're saying! What's the matter with you, boy? You deaf? Brain damaged?

LES:
> She knows.

FINESTAD:
> She knows but is she going to say?

LES *(looking up):*
> You know.

FINESTAD:
> That's right. I know.

LES:
> Well, you're the police, aren't you?

FINESTAD:
> That's right, I'm the police.

LES:
> So if you say I didn't do it—

FINESTAD:
> What do you think that means? You think I make the law? I don't make the law! *(He picks up the statute book, slams it on the desk)* I don't make the bloody law, Les! *(Pause, breathing heavily. When he speaks again it is quietly, with restraint)* What you did—you think that doesn't constitute an offence? What made you think you had the right?

LES:
> Taking it from them for as long as I can remember, that gave me the right.

FINESTAD:
> Les, the only rights we have are the rights the law gives us.

LES:
> Then fuck the law. One day I wake up and I say enough's enough. The sun's not going to shine clear through me and out the other side any longer. You can't make me believe that what I did was so terrible bad. I only settled accounts, didn't I?

FINESTAD:
> I'm not in charge of accounting. That's somebody else's department.

LES:

> But you turn me over to them—you know they'll make me
> pay twice over. Guys like me always do.

FINESTAD:

> I thought . . . I hoped it might have happened differently.
> Now I have no choice.

LES:

> Meaning?

FINESTAD:

> I have to lay a charge. *(Pause)* Maybe indecent assault.

LES *(softly, earnestly):*

> Don't give me away to them.

FINESTAD *looks guiltily at his hands.*

LES:

> That's what you asked when your back went out.
> That's what you asked *me*.

FINESTAD:

> It's the law.

LES *(stubbornly):*

> Don't give me away to them, please.

FINESTAD *(trying to justify himself):*

> Indecent assault is the best I can do, goddamn it!
> Tolbertson's demanding attempted rape!

LES *(stretching out his arms in exactly the same manner that*
FINESTAD *had to him earlier in the evening):*

> Don't do it.

FINESTAD *gets to his feet, springs around the desk, and forces* **LES'S**
arms down to his sides:

Stop it! Stop this foolishness! There's nothing else I can do! (**LES** *passively submits but when* **FINESTAD** *releases him he holds his hands out to him again*)

FINESTAD *rushes past him to the door, throws it open and shouts into the corridor.*

FINESTAD:
Heasman! Heasman! *Heasman!*

HEASMAN *(the sound of running, voice off):*
Coming! Coming, Sergeant!

HEASMAN *bursts into the office, anticipating trouble.*

FINESTAD *(to* **HEASMAN,** *turning his back on the boy with his hands held out to him):*
Get him out of here.

HEASMAN:
Sergeant?

FINESTAD *(turning on* **HEASMAN** *fiercely):*
Goddamn it, I said get him out of here!

HEASMAN:
Get him where, Sergeant?

FINESTAD:
Just out of here! Somewhere! Throw him in a holding cell!

HEASMAN *(with a look of satisfaction):*
All right, Sergeant! *(to* **LES***)* Come along, sonny.

LES *(disregarding* **HEASMAN,** *speaking only to* **FINESTAD***):*
Please.

HEASMAN *(seizing hold of* **LES'S** *arm):*
Come along.

LES *(as if suddenly aware of* **HEASMAN'S** *presence):*
No. *(Beat)* Please don't give me away to them.

HEASMAN:
Guess what? You don't have a choice in the matter.

LES *tries to pull himself free from* **HEASMAN'S** *grip. A struggle ensues and he is dragged towards the door shouting to* **FINESTAD** *who keeps his back turned to him.*

LES *(hysterical):*
Don't give me away to them! Please! Don't give me away to them!

HEASMAN *(twisting an arm behind* **LES'S** *back):*
Simmer down, sunshine. *(He pushes him through the doorway and the two disappear to the sounds of scuffling)*

FINESTAD *(swinging around and hurrying to the doorway):*
Don't hurt him! Go easy, for God's sake!

LES *continues to cry out in protest. The commotion diminishes. A door is heard to slam.*

FINESTAD *remains poised in the door until all is quiet once more. He turns back into the office and carefully, softly, closes the door behind him. He appears lost, returns to his desk, seats himself, absent-mindedly lights a cigarette and stares off into space. Suddenly, he takes the statute book, begins flipping pages, muttering to himself:*
Indecent assault, indecent assault, indecent assault. Here. *(Reads aloud)* "The accused in R. v. JONES, [1964] 2 C.C.C. 123, 41 C.R. 359, was charged with indecent assault and it was held that *any* physical contact in the circumstances of indecency was sufficient to constitute "indecent assault." *(The crash of a steel cell door freezes him. Unable to concentrate, he looks up from the book somewhat bewildered. Starts to read again, slowly)* "The accused in R. v. JONES, [1964] 2 C.C.C. 123, 41 C.R. 359, was charged with indecent assault . . . *(voice trails off into nothingness, sits staring into space. Rouses himself, grabs the statute book again, turns pages)* Indecent

83

assault— *(reads)* "Every one who indecently assaults a fe-
male person is guilty of an indictable offence and is liable to
imprisonment for five years and to be whipped." *(Not grasp-
ing what he reads)* Anyone who indecently assaults . . . is
guilty . . . to be whipped. *(Turns pages once again. Reads)*
"Every one who attempts to commit rape is guilty of an indictable offence and is liable to imprisonment for *(emphasis)*
ten years and to be whipped." *(Lets the book fall)* So the difference is . . . *(mentally computing)* ten for attempted rape and
five for indecent assault and whipping for both, which
makes the real difference . . . FINESTAD *ponders this, then,
abruptly, and with an air of finality he strides to the desk, picks up
the telephone and dials.*

FINESTAD:
 Tom, you're still there? Please come to the office.

*He sets down the phone and stands behind the desk waiting, looking
calm and resolved. There is a tap at the door and* HEASMAN *steps
into the office.*

HEASMAN:
 Yes?

FINESTAD:
 Is he quiet now?

HEASMAN:
 More or less.

FINESTAD:
 All right then. If he's quiet release him.

HEASMAN:
 Release him?

FINESTAD:
 That's what I said. Release him. *(Taps his watch)* It's five
 o'clock. We wouldn't want to make him late for work.

HEASMAN:
> For a minute, just a minute, I thought you'd seen the light.

FINESTAD:
> The light? Who knows?

HEASMAN:
> No charges?

FINESTAD:
> There'll likely be charges. But not from me.

HEASMAN:
> Then I might as well say goodbye to you right now. *(He laughs in disbelief)* I've never seen a man take such trouble to shoot himself in the foot.

FINESTAD:
> The aim is all important, Tom.

HEASMAN:
> Why, Jack? Why self-destruct?

FINESTAD:
> Well, I suppose back trouble's part of it.

HEASMAN:
> Back trouble?

FINESTAD:
> Yes, chiefly trouble in that location. Not further north as some would like to think.

HEASMAN *shakes his head, uncertain what to make of* **FINESTAD**.

FINESTAD:
> When I consulted the book I found it wasn't very helpful, wasn't very clear at all. What does it mean, exactly, that "any physical contact in the circumstances of indecency is

sufficient to constitute indecent assault"? Can you make head or tail of that? So I said to myself, When the answers aren't supplied by the book, what's a poor ordinary, dumb cop to do but throw up his hands.

HEASMAN:
It's got nothing to do with the book.

FINESTAD:
No? But I've been a man of the book, and a man should attempt to make excuses appear consistent with the beginning, middle, and end of his career.

HEASMAN:
You really think this is the end?

FINESTAD *(mildly)*:
Maybe it should be. *(Pause)* At the very least Tolbertson will see that I'm transferred.

HEASMAN:
So is putting a burr under Tolbertson's foreskin worth getting the push? Because that's what all this is about, isn't it?

FINESTAD:
Not any more it isn't. Something broke down tonight, Tom. Either the book, or me. I'm not sure which. *(Pause)* You won't believe what was just in my mind.

HEASMAN *(sympathetically)*:
What?

FINESTAD:
A goddamn poem.

HEASMAN:
A poem? You?

FINESTAD:
> Didn't they make you learn poems when you went to school? They did us.

HEASMAN *looks bewildered.*

FINESTAD *(remembering):*
> Grade three. Miss Knight. *(Suddenly)* "Tyger! Tyger! burning bright / In the forests of the night." Know what that makes me think of?

HEASMAN *shakes his head.*

FINESTAD:
> Les Grant. In the pump room. Watching them dance. "Tyger! Tyger! burning bright . . ."

HEASMAN *doesn't speak.*

FINESTAD:
> I remember . . . the guy who wrote this poem . . . he kept asking: Who made the tiger? Who made the tiger?

HEASMAN *(quizzically):*
> Yes?

FINESTAD:
> Who made Les Grant? *(Answers himself)* They did. And who made that girl? More of the same. *(Beat)* Poor, sorry, fucked-up tigers. And you and me—we're supposed to play tiger tamer. After they've used their teeth. I might have been up to the game—once. But all of a sudden it seems too complicated for rules—for me. *(Pause)* I know what the boy did was wrong. But how wrong? Ten years? Five? *(Shrugs because he has no answers)*

HEASMAN:
> So what are you saying?

FINESTAD:
> Just that the more I learned the harder I found it was to
> pass judgement—on either of those kids. *(Beat)* They
> tell us God knows all our reasons. Maybe that's why
> He's supposed to find it easier to forgive than the rest
> of us.

HEASMAN:
> You aren't God. You can't save him.

FINESTAD:
> True. All I know is that if Tolbertson and me had
> ganged up on a kid like Les Grant, any book definition—
> indecent assault, attempted rape—would have stuck.

HEASMAN:
> And now?

FINESTAD:
> It's up in the air. Where justice probably always is . . .
> up in the air. *(Pause)* Maybe I'm talking nonsense.
> I'm tired. It's time for me to go home. When you're
> my age a shift and a half takes it out of you. I've got
> church soon.

HEASMAN:
> Can we shake hands now, or do I wait until you
> officially get your walking papers?

FINESTAD *(surprised)*:
> Whichever you prefer.

HEASMAN:
> I'd like to be the first to say goodbye. In private.
> *(He holds out his hand)*

The two men shake hands solemnly. **FINESTAD** *suddenly
throws his arm over* **HEASMAN'S** *shoulder and gives him
an affectionate squeeze. It is over very quickly, the two men
separate sheepishly.*

FINESTAD *(laughing at how they must look):*
> It'll be a while yet before you're rid of me. Things
> don't move that quickly.

HEASMAN:
> Still. Beat the rush. Like shopping before Christmas.
> *(Pause. Attempting optimism)* Who knows how it'll
> turn out?

FINESTAD:
> For all concerned.

HEASMAN:
> That's right. For all concerned.

Pause.

HEASMAN:
> Goodnight, Sergeant.

They separate. **HEASMAN** *exits.* **FINESTAD** *remains in the*
doorway with his hand on the light switch.

FINESTAD *(to himself):*
> And good morning. *(Beat)* There's still confession to come.

He switches off the light, stands silhouetted in the doorway,
then departs.

Curtain.

About the Author

Guy Vanderhaeghe has published fiction in some of the best periodicals in the world, including the *London Review of Books, The Chelsea Journal, Canadian Fiction Magazine, Saturday Night, The Malahat Review,* and *London Magazine.* His work has been included in the anthologies *Modern Stories in English, The Oxford Book of Canadian Short Stories in English, The Houghton Mifflin Anthology of Short Fiction, The Bridge City Anthology: Stories from Saskatoon, The Norton Anthology of Contemporary Fiction,* and many others. His previous books include *Man Descending, The Trouble with Heroes, My Present Age,* and *Homesick.* He lives in Saskatoon with his wife, Margaret.